D1308544

COMMUNICATION Inventions

THE TALK OF THE TOWN

Alexander Offord

Crabtree Publishing Company

www.crabtreebooks.com

JEFFERSONVILLE TOWNSHIP PUBLIC LIBRARY
JEFFERSONVILLE, INDIANA
BRANCH COLLECTION
JUL - - 2014

INVENTIONS THAT SHAPED THE MODERN WORLD

Author: Alexander Offord
Publishing plan research and development:
　Reagan Miller
Editors: Helen Mason, Rachel Eagen
Copy editor: Janice Dyer
Proofreader: Dimitra Chronopoulos
Editorial services: Clarity Content Services
Design: Pixel Hive Studio
Cover design: Samara Parent
Photo research: Linda Tanaka
Project coordinator and prepress technician:
　Samara Parent
Print coordinator: Margaret Amy Salter
Series consultants:
Professor D. Eric Walters, Ph.D.
　Rosalind Franklin University of Medicine and Science
Jane Hutchison, Masters of Education

Cover: Vintage 1930's Philco radio (middle);
Telecommunication antenna (right); woman working
on a laptop computer and talking on a cell phone (bottom left)
Back cover: Vintage crank telephone

Photographs: front cover middle R. Gino Santa
Maria/shutterstock, right Jakrit Jiraratwaro/shutterstock,
bottom left John Warner/shutterstock; p1 Rido/shutterstock;
back cover p4 cowardlion/shutterstock; p5 Oleksiy
Mark/shutterstock; p7 Jeff Ogden/CCL; p8 GTS
Production/shutterstock; p10 left Michal Manas/CCL, Erick
Margarita Images/shutterstock; p11 Hemera/Thinkstock; p12
upstudio/shutterstock; p13 NYC Wanderer/Kevin Eng/CCL;
p14 LC-USZ62-30750/Library of Congress Prints and
Photographs Division Washington, D.C. 20540 USA; p16
Barry Barnes/shutterstock; p17 left Photos.com/Thinkstock,
Georgios Kollidas/shutterstock; p18 villorejo/shutterstock;
p21 left cristi180884/shutterstock, Kou07kou/CCL; p22
Photo courtesy of Valeria Vito; p23 "Alexander Graham Bell
at the opening of the long-distance line from New York to
Chicago," 1892. Prints and Photographs Division, Library of
Congress. Reproduction Number LC-G9-Z2-28608-B; p28
LC-USZ62-109738 Library of Congress, Radio-Craft
Magazine January 1930 Photo courtesy of Frederick Jaggi;
p32 SPL/Science Source; p34 Thomas Klee/shutterstock; p35
Bruno Barral (ByB)/CCL; p37 top Photo Courtesy of Texas
Instruments, iStockphoto/Thinkstock; p38 Hstoff/CCL; p39
John S. and James L. Knight Foundation/CCL; p40 right
iStockphoto/Thinkstock; p41 REUTERS/Morris Mac Matzen;
p42 iStockphoto/Thinkstock.

Library and Archives Canada Cataloguing in Publication

Offord, Alexander, author
　　Communication inventions : the talk of the town / Alexander Offord.

(Inventions that shaped the modern world)
Includes index.
Issued in print and electronic formats.
ISBN 978-0-7787-0222-1 (bound).--ISBN 978-0-7787-0235-1 (pbk.)
ISBN 978-1-4271-9421-3 (html).--ISBN 978-1-4271-9425-1 (pdf)

　　1. Communication--Technological innovations--Juvenile literature.
I. Title.

P96.T42O44 2013　　　　j302.2　　　　C2013-906240-8
　　　　　　　　　　　　　　　　　　　　　　　C2013-906241-6

Library of Congress Cataloging-in-Publication Data

CIP available at Library of Congress

Crabtree Publishing Company

Printed in Canada/102013/BF20130920

www.crabtreebooks.com　　　　1-800-387-7650

Copyright © **2014 CRABTREE PUBLISHING COMPANY.** All rights reserved. No part of this publication may be reproduced,
stored in a retrieval system or be transmitted in any form or by any means, electronic, mechanical, photocopying, recording, or
otherwise, without the prior written permission of Crabtree Publishing Company. In Canada: We acknowledge the financial support
of the Government of Canada through the Canada Book Fund for our publishing activities.

**Published in
Canada
Crabtree Publishing**
616 Welland Ave.
St. Catharines, ON
L2M 5V6

**Published in the
United States
Crabtree Publishing**
PMB 59051
350 Fifth Avenue, 59th Floor
New York, New York 10118

**Published in the
United Kingdom
Crabtree Publishing**
Maritime House
Basin Road North, Hove
BN41 1WR

**Published in
Australia
Crabtree Publishing**
3 Charles Street
Coburg North
VIC, 3058

Contents

Human Beings Are Social

Did you know that the average person speaks about 150 words a minute? Or that every day, 294 billion emails are sent all over the world? That's about 3.4 million each second. Over 12 billion telephone calls are made each day, and 6 billion text messages are exchanged. As if that weren't enough, we also send 3 billion letters through the mail each year.

Human beings love to communicate. **Communication** is the exchange of ideas, stories, and information. Each day we pass on news, ideas, and information to our neighbors, family, and friends. We send and receive messages around the world. As a result of advanced **technologies**, an email or instant message can travel across the globe in a heartbeat. Communicating is very important to our well-being.

For about 192,000 years, humans communicated with each other by talking face-to-face. Writing is a relatively recent **invention**. In the past 150 years, we have developed faster ways to communicate over long distances. To do this, innovative people invented various forms of communication technology.

Inventions and Innovations Solve Problems

We develop technology when we use a scientific **discovery** to make new tools to solve problems. A discovery is when someone uncovers something new about the world for the first time. For example, in 1750 Benjamin Franklin discovered that lightning was made of electricity.

A new piece of technology can either be an invention or an **innovation**.

- An invention is a process, machine, or device that has been made for the first time. For example, Alexander Graham Bell invented the telephone, the first device capable of sending the human voice across a great distance.

- Innovations occur when an existing invention is improved or changed by using new discoveries or in response to a new need. For example, in 1973 Martin D. Cooper created a telephone that worked through **radio waves** rather than using wires. This was the first cell phone. In 1992, a Canadian named Neil Papworth discovered how to send text messages from a cell phone.

Innovations constantly change and improve inventions.

From crank phones (left) to smartphones (right), we've come a long way.

The Earliest Inventions

The first important communication invention in history was writing. The oldest forms of writing come from Mesopotamia, which is known as the Middle East today. In Mesopotamia around 4000 BCE, a people called the Sumerians began scratching marks in clay. The scratches could be combined in different ways to tell a story. This was called **cuneiform** writing. Cuneiform was the first alphabet ever created.

← This letter was written in cuneiform around 2400 BCE to inform a king of his son's death.

Writing has been around for so long, it's easy for us to take it for granted. For the Sumerians, writing was as exciting an invention as smartphones are for us today. In this book, you will learn about the history of communication, from cuneiform to email. We've come a long way since ancient Mesopotamia, and there have been some bumps along the road. These difficulties inspired many inventors, including Samuel Morse who invented the **telegraph**.

The following quotation was written by a Greek philosopher who knew a lot about inventors and inventing.

"Necessity is the mother of invention"

— Plato

Inventors Look for Solutions

What Plato meant was that inventions and innovations occur because inventors think they can solve a problem. We don't know who invented cuneiform. But we do know why it was invented. As Sumerian cities grew bigger, it became harder for merchants to keep track of where their goods were going. They needed a way to record their transactions. Cuneiform was the solution.

As you read this book, you will see how the most amazing solutions can sometimes come from surprising places. You will see how a young man born in a log cabin with no electricity invented television. You will read how a deaf newspaper salesman discovered how to record music, and how a painter invented a way to send messages all over the world.

Great inventors come from many different backgrounds. They all share certain characteristics. They are determined, curious, creative, and self-reliant. Inventing takes a lot of hard work. It isn't always easy; however, inventors who have persevered have changed our world.

↓ *This map shows the number of people that use the Internet. The dark blue countries have the highest number of Internet users.*

| 100M |
| 20M |
| 10M |
| 5M |
| 2M |
| 1M |
| 500K |
| 100K |
| 20K |
| 0 |
| No data |

CHAPTER ONE

The Written Word

Today, most of us learn to read and write soon after we start school. Until about 1870, only boys of wealthy families learned to read and write. They either went to school or had tutors who taught them at home.

In ancient societies, people who could read and write were given special jobs in the royal courts. They were called **scribes**.

It took hundreds of years and the work of many great inventors to bring reading and writing to the whole world. Amazing inventions such as paper and the **printing press** are what allow so many people to read and write today. Although we know the names of most of the later inventors, we don't know who invented the first alphabet or the first method of writing.

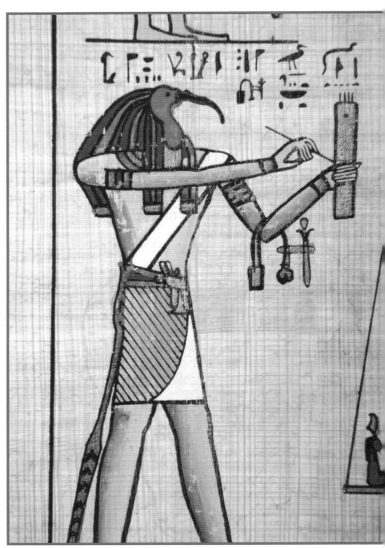

↑ This ancient Egyptian painting shows a scribe at work. He's holding an early version of the pencil, called a "**stylus**."

↑ *This Egyptian religious text is written on papyrus.*

The Invention of Paper

Everything we read is a combination of words that make sentences, and sentences that make paragraphs. This is called **text**. Text itself isn't difficult to create, as long as you know how to read and write. The problem is that in order to communicate ideas for others to read, people have to write on something.

We don't know who first tried to write. Perhaps people started by making marks in the dirt to pass messages back and forth. We do know that Egyptian scribes wrote on clay tablets. These tablets could be as big as a tombstone or as small as a saucer. When the clay was soft, the writer made scratches in it with a piece of reed or bamboo, called a stylus. The earliest tablets we have are business records, such as receipts and bills.

Clay tablets were very heavy and difficult to carry. This made traveling with them extremely difficult. It was also nearly impossible to store them. Imagine a library filled with huge slabs of clay!

In the year 3000 BCE, the Ancient Egyptian Empire was very large and powerful. It took a lot of careful record-keeping to run an empire that big. To make things easier, the Egyptians invented the earliest form of paper, called **papyrus**.

9

Papyrus, the First Paper

Some ingenious Egyptian wove together the dried leaves of the papyrus plant, making a thin sheet of papyrus, the world's first paper. Maybe the same person squeezed the plant's stem to make a juice. The juice mixed with water made the first ink. Egyptian scribes dipped a stylus in this ink and then wrote on the papyrus.

→ *Papyrus is a water plant that grows along rivers throughout Africa.*

Animal Skins Provide Parchment

Around 200 BCE, the Greeks began using animal skins to make a longer-lasting form of paper. To make **parchment** paper, they soaked animal skins in water for a day. Then they poured fermented juice made from rotting vegetables over the skins. This loosened the hair, which they scraped off. They then stretched the skins until they were very thin.

← *Here, a goatskin is being stretched and dried to make parchment.*

In 105 CE, the Chinese inventor Ts'ai Lun made paper from rags and plant fibers that he soaked in water, mashed into a paste, and then spread out to dry. His invention didn't reach Europe until the 1100s. For 600 years, it would be the most popular paper.

Early Books

Books didn't always look the way they do today. The first books were rolled-up pieces of papyrus or parchment, called **scrolls**. Scrolls were very delicate. In 200 CE, the Romans invented a book with a front and back cover and pages in between. We still use this type of book, called a **codex**.

Until 1450, books were written by hand. For this reason, they were precious. Only the very rich and powerful could afford them.

Gutenberg's Great Invention

The world changed in 1440. That's when a man named Johannes Gutenberg finished his invention of the printing press. This press was like a giant stamp. It used small tiles to print words. Each tile had a letter, and each letter was dipped in ink and set into place on the press. Then the press pushed the letters down on a piece of paper.

→ *This carving shows a monk hard at work. Imagine working day after day, month after month, copying out every word in the Bible. How long do you think that would take? The printing press eliminated jobs like this.*

Gutenberg's Printing Press

Gutenburg didn't comment on the difficulties he had using his printing press, but people who used it later did. Everything on the page is laid out backwards. All of the letters are backwards too. The quotation below shows the way a sentence appeared on Gutenberg's press.

→ *This re-creation of Gutenberg's printing press was built in 2009.*

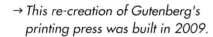

" .grednetuG ot ewo ti ,dab dna doog ,yad-ot si dlrow eht tahW "

Put this page up to a mirror to read what Mark Twain had to say in 1900 about Gutenberg's invention.

Johannes Gutenberg

Johannes Gutenberg (1395–1468) was born in Mainz, Germany. Little is known about his early life. His father worked in a mint, and as a result, the young Gutenberg grew up learning how to melt gold to make jewelry and coins. Between 1439 and 1450, he lived in the city of Strasbourg. We don't know what he did there; however, that's when he invented his great printing press.

Gutenberg's Bible

In 1454, Gutenberg printed the famous Gutenberg Bible. The Bible was in Latin and was used in churches during mass. Today, the ones that still exist are in museums all over the world, including in the United States, Spain, Portugal, Russia, Japan, Germany, Austria, and England.

↑ *This Gutenberg Bible is in the New York Public Library. Today, one of the original Bibles is worth $35 million.*

Gutenberg's Legacy

Gutenberg's printing press changed the way people communicate. Books no longer had to be written by hand. Many copies could be made much more quickly and easily. More books were made. They became cheaper to buy, and soon more people could afford them. Since there were more books around, more people learned to read.

Once more people could read, Gutenberg's press was used to make pamphlets, flyers, and newsletters, as well as books. Information could be spread much more easily.

Gutenberg didn't invent the *first* printing press. The very first was invented by the Chinese inventor Bì Shēng, sometime between 1041 and 1048. Bì Shēng's press was much simpler than Gutenberg's. It used ceramic tiles instead of metal ones, and was operated by hand instead of a machine.

"It is a press, certainly, but a press from which shall flow... A spring of truth [to] ... scatter the darkness of ignorance...."

— Johannes Gutenberg, 1436

CHAPTER TWO

Great Leaps Forward

A big challenge for inventors was how to send messages over a great distance. We don't know who the first person was to use fires to signal an emergency. These were often used in wartime to send warnings about approaching enemies. More detailed messages were delivered on foot, by boat, or on horseback, such as Paul Revere's famous ride in 1775.

After Gutenberg's printing press, 300 years went by before the next big step in communication. However, other discoveries were made during that time.

In 1750, the American scientist and politician Benjamin Franklin discovered how to harness electricity by flying a kite with a metal key during a thunderstorm.

It took more than 85 years for someone to figure out how to apply this discovery to communication. Then, several inventors made electric telegraphs. Then came the invention of the typewriter. This was developed in 1808 by an Italian who wanted to help someone he loved write letters, even though she couldn't see.

← Franklin proved that electricity could be harnessed with metal. This discovery allowed people to use electricity in machines such as the telegraph.

→ *The location of the arms on the top of this semaphore station communicates a letter. In this way, operators passed messages from one tower to the next. These arms show the letter Q.*

The Telegraph

Communicating words to a distant place was invented by a Frenchman named Claude Chappe (1763–1805). Chappe lived during the French Revolution. At this time, the French people were overthrowing their king and nobles. The government asked Chappe to invent a system that would allow them to receive reports from their armies.

Chappe invented a system called **semaphore**. This system used a pair of mechanical arms placed in different positions to show letters that spelled words. The wooden arms were located on the top of towers so they could be seen from a distance. An operator in one tower spelled out a message. An operator in the next tower translated it and passed it on to the next tower. In this way, messages could travel long distances.

In 1794, Chappe gave these towers the name telegraph, which comes from the Greek words for "far" (*tele*) and "writing" (*graphia*).

The Limits of Chappe's Telegraph

Chappe's mechanical telegraph was a big improvement over using messengers. Information could be transmitted over long distances much more quickly. However, there were some problems.

- The system relied on the ability of tower operators to see their nearest neighbor. This meant that no messages could be sent at night or in bad weather.

- The mechanical arms had to be operated by hand. This made it very difficult to send messages in a hurry.

- Anyone who knew the semaphore alphabet could read the message, including spies.

Semaphore is still used. For example, people use flags to pass on messages on navy vessels and in mountainous places where electronic communication is difficult.

→ *This semaphore alphabet is based on Chappe's semaphore. Try it with a friend. Can you send and read each other's messages?*

The First Electric Telegraph

The drawbacks of Chappe's invention were solved by the first electric telegraph. This was built in 1837 by two British inventors, William Cooke (1806 – 1879) and Charles Wheatstone (1802 –1875). Their **five-needle telegraph** used pulses of electricity to move a series of needles on a board. There were letters on the board. Depending on the number of pulses, the needle would point to a different letter to spell out a word.

Imagine the excitement when this invention was used to catch a criminal! On January 1, 1845, James Tawell was arrested at England's Paddington train station when a telegram was sent to the police from Slough Station. It read:

A MURDER HAS GUST BEEN COMMITTED AT SALT HILL AND THE SUSPECTED MURDERER WAS SEEN TO TAKE A FIRST CLASS TICKET TO LONDON BY THE TRAIN WHICH LEFT SLOUGH AT 742 PM HE IS IN THE GARB OF A KWAKER WITH A GREAT COAT ON WHICH REACHES NEARLY DOWN TO HIS FEET HE IS IN THE LAST COMPARTMENT OF THE SECOND CLASS COMPARTMENT

This was the first time that a telegram had helped the police. It would not be the last.

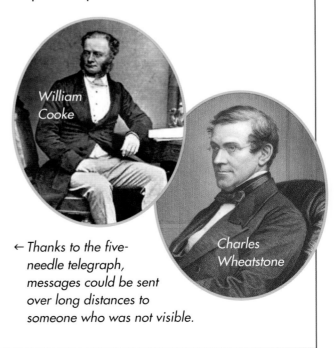

William Cooke

Charles Wheatstone

← Thanks to the five-needle telegraph, messages could be sent over long distances to someone who was not visible.

← Samuel Morse

↓ Morse's telegraph sent messages faster than the one invented by Cooke and Wheatstone. It was also less expensive.

Samuel Morse

Another invention could send messages even faster. Samuel Finley Breese Morse (1791 –1872) was born in Charlestown, Massachusetts. He eventually went to study at Yale College. There, he studied painting, but also went to lectures on electricity. After he graduated from Yale, Morse went to England to study art. It was there that he was first introduced to the idea of **telegraphy**. This is the study of using or making systems to communicate information.

The event that spurred Morse to improve the telegraph happened in 1825 when he was back in America. He was asked to do a portrait for a French nobleman. He went to New York to get started.

While there, he received a message from a postman riding on horseback. It was from his father, saying that Morse's wife was very sick. By the time Morse got back to New Haven, Connecticut, she had died.

If he had received the message sooner, he might have been able to get home in time to say goodbye to his wife. Morse wanted to prevent his tragedy from happening to others. For this reason, he dedicated his life to developing a faster way of delivering messages. It took him 12 years to figure out how to do it. In 1837, he completed his invention of the **Morse code** telegraph, but didn't get to use it for another seven years.

Morse Code

Morse invented a special alphabet for his machine, called Morse code. Using this code, people sent messages by turning the letters into electric pulses. These pulses moved a needle that drew dots and lines on a piece of paper. Then someone translated the code back into letters.

The first message was sent from Washington to Baltimore on May 24, 1844. Morse let his friend's daughter, Annie Ellsworth, choose the wording for that first message. She picked the following line from the Bible.

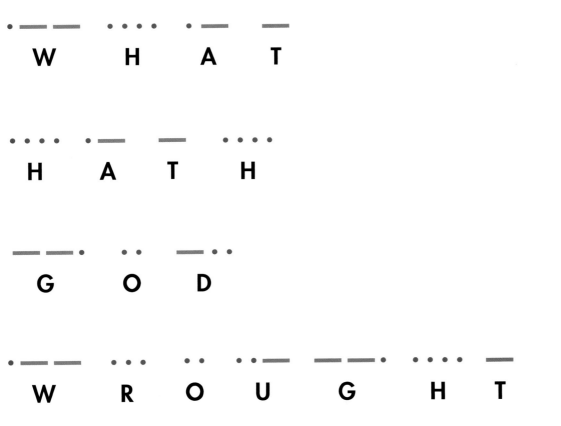

Although Morse's system was much faster than a man on horseback, it also had its drawbacks. The person sending the messages had to know Morse code. So did the receiver. Also, messages were sent over an electric wire. If the wire was broken, messages stopped.

Inventions for the Blind

The telegraph allowed people to send and receive messages, even though they couldn't see each other. In the 1800s, inventors began to apply these ideas to help the blind.

The Typewriter

The first typewriter was invented around 1808 by an Italian named Pellegrino Turri. Turri was a romantic young man. When the woman he loved lost her sight, Turri developed a way to help her. He thought that it would be easier for her to write letters if she didn't have to write by hand. To help, he invented the first typewriter, a machine that wrote by pushing buttons, or keys.

After Turri's invention, other inventors created a few other kinds of typewriter, but none became popular. This changed in 1873, when a poet and inventor named Christopher Sholes (1819–1890) invented the qwerty keyboard. Take a look at a computer keyboard. The top row of letters begins q-w-e-r-t-y. The letters were placed in that order on the advice of telegraph operators. The operators had to type and translate messages from Morse code. Placing certain letters near each other made this job easier and quicker.

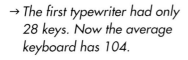
→ *The first typewriter had only 28 keys. Now the average keyboard has 104.*

The Braille Alphabet

Turri wasn't the only person to make things to help the blind. In 1821, a 12-year-old boy from France invented the **Braille alphabet**. People who lose one sense are often able to strengthen others. For example, those who are blind often have a delicate sense of touch. Louis Braille used a series of six raised dots to make letters. By using their fingertips, people without sight can feel the dots and read.

By 1824, when he was 15, Braille had finished his entire alphabet. What inspired him? Louis Braille was blind.

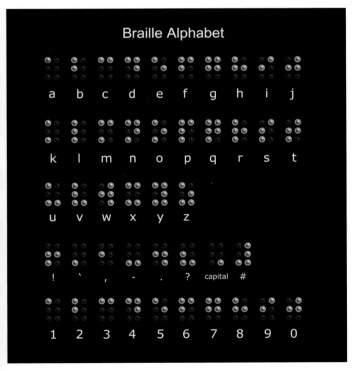

↑ *This photo shows the complete Braille alphabet. The next time you're in an elevator, check out the floor indicators. Each number is in regular writing and Braille.*

Louis Braille

Louis Braille (1809–1852) was born in a small town near Paris. When he was three, he hurt his eye on an awl. This is a sharp, needle-like tool used to make holes in leather. The wound became infected, and he lost his sight. Fortunately, Paris had a famous school for the blind where Braille studied and invented his alphabet.

Today, this alphabet is used in books and on public signs.

CHAPTER THREE

The Spoken Word

Imagine if you could listen to a song only when it is performed live. Or imagine not knowing what the leader of your country's voice sounds like. This was the norm for most of human history. During that time, the only way to hear someone's voice was to be nearby.

Starting in the 1850s, three exciting discoveries changed that. First, one man learned how to throw the human voice great distances. Then another discovered how to turn a song into something you can hold in your hand. Finally, a third invented a way to communicate over great distances without wires.

What Came Before the Telephone?

The telephone has a long history. The technology was first developed by an Italian named Innocenzo Manzetti (1826–1877). In 1865, he used telegraph wires to make it sound as though a toy robot was talking.

→ *This is one of Manzetti's automatons. As you can see from the position of the arms, it was built to play the flute. If he had realized the potential of his robot innovation, Manzetti might have invented the first telephone or phonograph.*

The First Telephone

Other inventors saw the potential of Manzetti's idea. One of them was Alexander Graham Bell (1847–1922).

Bell was born in Edinburgh, Scotland. When he was 12 years old, his mother began to lose her hearing. Bell studied sound to learn more about deafness. As he learned, Bell taught people who could not hear or speak. During this time, he also worked on his telephone.

When he was 23, Bell moved to Canada. There he began working on an early version of his telephone. He also made up the word, *telephone*, which means to speak from a distance.

On March 10, 1876, Bell made the first phone call to his assistant, Thomas Watson. He got a **patent** for his invention later that year. A patent gives inventors the right to make, use, or sell their idea.

Although it took many years to put up the wires necessary to carry telephone messages, Bell's invention allowed for fast, efficient, person-to-person communication. Before the telephone, a personal message might take days by mail. Telegrams weren't very private.

↑ *Today, when people answer the telephone, they say "Hello?" Bell suggested answering with "Ahoy!" This was how sailors greeted ships at sea.*

Bell wasn't the only one working on a telephone. Italian inventor Antonio Meucci (1808 –1889) built his own versions in the 1850s. He didn't patent them because he felt they weren't finished. Otherwise, he would have been first.

Music Made Solid

For centuries, people have gathered to sing and play music together. Pianists were invited to dinner parties to give special concerts. Traveling orchestras played the newest hits. When these musicians left, the music ended until they returned. All that changed in 1877 when an American named Thomas Edison invented the **phonograph**.

The Phonograph

The phonograph, a device that earned him a worldwide reputation, was Edison's first invention. Like today's VCRs and PVRs, Edison's phonograph both recorded and played sound. It recorded sound through a stylus similar to what the early Egyptians used for writing.

Thomas Edison

Thomas Edison (1847–1931) was born in Milan, Ohio, the youngest of eleven children. Although he loved to read, he was a poor student. As a young boy, Edison got scarlet fever, a disease that made him almost deaf. When he grew older, he sold newspapers for a living and worked on inventions in his spare time.

By the end of his life in 1931, Edison held 1093 patents. We still use some of these today, including the incandescent light bulb. What was his secret?

↑ *This picture was taken in 1878, the year after Edison invented the phonograph.*

"We sometimes learn a lot from our failures, if we have put into the effort the best thought and work we are capable of."

— Thomas Edison, 1921

Edison's Invention

These drawings from the phonograph's patent papers show Edison's idea. His phonograph was the first device that could record sound. With his invention, a great symphony didn't have to end when the musicians went home. This phonograph is the ancestor of the modern iPod.

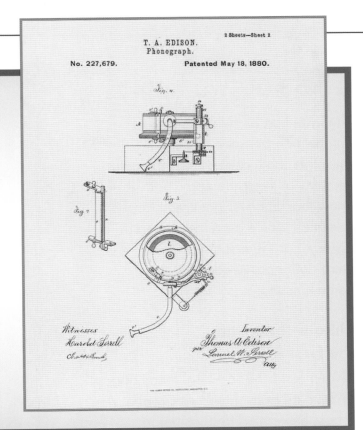

When someone made a sound, a mechanical device called a **diaphragm** vibrated. The stylus then made grooves in a sheet of tinfoil that was wrapped around a cylinder.

To play sound, the stylus was set back at the beginning of the groove on the tinfoil. When the cylinder turned, the stylus retraced the grooves. This made the diaphragm vibrate and reproduce the sound it had just recorded.

Later, the tinfoil was switched to wax, which was cheaper and made a clearer sound. The wax cylinders had to be stored in cool conditions or they would melt.

The oldest known recording of the human voice is from 1860. It is a phonograph cylinder of a man singing the French folk song "Au Clair de la Lune". Check out page 43 to find out where you can listen to it.

A Tale of Two Radios

The invention of the radio was a competition between two great inventors. Both of them had their own versions of the technology. Both knew that whoever got credit for the invention would be remembered in history. For the first time, wires were no longer needed for communication.

Nikola Tesla and the First Radio

Nikola Tesla (1856 –1943) was born in Smiljan, part of today's Croatia. As a boy, he wanted to become an engineer. His father was a minister and insisted that Tesla enter the priesthood. Fortunately for history, Tesla almost died of cholera when he was 17. After that, his father let him follow his dream.

Soon after graduating, Tesla traveled to America to work for Thomas Edison. In his spare time, he invented a way of transmitting and receiving radio waves. He applied for a patent in 1897. He gave his first demonstration in 1898.

Guglielmo Marconi and the First Radio Signals

Guglielmo Marconi (1874 –1937) was born in Bologna, Italy. Although he went

↑ Tesla used his invention to direct the first remote-controlled boat.

to the best schools, he was not a good student. However, he was very interested in science, especially the work of Heinrich Hertz.

In 1895, Marconi built a machine that could transmit radio waves over a great distance. In 1900, he patented this radio. In 1901, he sent the first radio signal from St. John's, Newfoundland, to Poldhu, England.

Heinrich Rudolf Hertz

Heinrich Rudolf Hertz (1856 –1894), was born in Hamburg, Germany. In 1886, while teaching at the University of Karlsruhe, he discovered that an electric field can be combined with a magnetic field to create an **electromagnetic field**. This is what radio waves are made of.

Two Inventors Claim the Same Title

There were two patents for two different radios. Tesla patented his radio first, but Marconi was a world famous celebrity. The patent office canceled Tesla's patent. Marconi became the official inventor of the radio.

Tesla sued Marconi.

Marconi . . . is using 17 of my patents.

— Nikola Tesla, 1901

Unfortunately, Tesla ran out of money and had to stop the lawsuit. Although he transmitted radio waves in 1897 and Marconi didn't make his first transmission until 1901, Marconi was known around the world as the inventor of the radio.

In 1943, the U.S. Supreme Court overturned the patent office's decision. This ruling reinstated Tesla as the inventor of the radio. Tesla died that year.

↓ *Marconi's radio message was the letter s in Morse code.*

The Radio's Significance

Radio technology is one of the most important inventions of the 1900s. It allowed people in England to hear music being played in New York. Sporting events could be narrated over the radio. People who couldn't afford tickets could join in the fun. Ships could call for help, making sea voyages safer. News of the world could be transmitted right into people's homes.

↑ *Families were fascinated by the news, music, and drama they heard on the early radio.*

The invention of the radio led to wireless Internet, cell phones, and satellite television.

Reginald Fessenden
Radio's First Voice

The first person to broadcast a human voice over the radio was Reginald Fessenden (1866–1932). Fessenden was a Canadian inventor born in Sherbrooke, Quebec. Before Marconi's radio, he came up with the idea of using radio waves to send sound. In 1900, he invented a special generator that allowed sound waves to be carried on radio waves. On December 24, 1906, he made the first voice broadcast.

Reginald Fessenden

↑ *The first radio program was a Christmas concert beamed to ships in the Atlantic Ocean and the Caribbean.*

CHAPTER FOUR

From Still Pictures to Moving Ones

Cave paintings likely told stories.

The earliest form of communication was through pictures. The oldest known pictures are in the Cave of El Castillo, in Spain. They are over 40,000 years old.

Over time, paintings on cave walls evolved into paintings on paper, canvas, and tiles. In the 1600s, the first projector was built. The machine was called a magic lantern, and worked by channeling light down a small hole and through a glass slide. This projected a static image on a wall.

In the 1800s, **photography** became popular. Photography uses light to take pictures. The first pictures were made on glass plates covered in silver salts that absorbed light and made an image. Innovative people gradually figured out how to make pictures that could move.

↑ *It took almost ten minutes to take the first photos. That's why everyone looks so stiff. Notice the stand that holds the man in place while his picture is being taken.*

The first camera was invented by the Arab scholar Ibn al-Haytham in the 800s. The camera filtered light through a pinhole. The light struck a mirror inside; the mirror projected the image.

The Birth of Cinema

A movie camera works by rapidly taking many pictures. The pictures are then run through a projector at high speeds. The film to make these kinds of pictures was invented before there was a way to show them.

Celluloid Film

In 1888, an American inventor named George Eastman (1854–1932) invented **celluloid film**. Celluloid is a very thin plastic that was cheaper than glass. It could be rolled up inside a camera. This allowed people to take pictures much faster, an ability that led to moving pictures.

→ *This child's flip book from 1886 has a series of still pictures that show small amounts of body movement. Flipping through the pages gives the impression of movement. Movies are also a series of still pictures shown at high speed.*

The Movie Camera

In 1889, a British photographer named William Friese-Green (1855–1921) built the first movie camera. This camera could take ten pictures a second. At first, he used an oil-coated film. When he learned about celluloid, he tried the new film, which worked much better.

Thomas Edison also made a movie camera in 1889. His innovation was called the **kinetoscope** and had a built-in projector.

Auguste (left) and
Louis (right) Lumière

↑ *The Lumière brothers' most famous movie was The Arrival of a Train at La Ciotat Station. When they first showed it, the audience screamed in fear. They thought a train was driving toward them from the screen.*

The Lumière Brothers

By 1890, people had the equipment to make movies. It took two French brothers to figure out how to use it for entertainment. Auguste Lumière (1862–1954) was born in Bescançon, France. He was very close to his younger brother, Louis (1864–1948). The boys' father was a professional photographer who sold photographic supplies. After studying science at the local school, the pair started to work for their father. While working, they invented new ways to take pictures and develop film.

The Lumière brothers used Edison's and Friese-Green's technology to tell stories.

In 1892, they built their own version of the kinetoscope. Their camera was called the **cinematoscope**. In 1895, these brothers used their camera to make longer movies that told stories. Their idea led to the cinema as we know it today.

Today, the movie industry makes $35 billion a year. Louis Lumière would be quite surprised. After all, he thought that:

Cinema is an invention without a future.

— Louis Lumière, 1895

Turning on the Television

It took imagination to figure out how to put moving pictures in a small box that people could watch at home. The person who succeeded was a Scotsman named John Logie Baird (1888–1946). Baird wanted to create a kind of telephone where people could see each other. His system used radio technology. It could run on its own using a motor to generate power. The motor spun a disk charged with electric pulses to create images. The disk spun so fast that it seemed the images were moving.

Baird first demonstrated this invention on January 26, 1926.

↑ *This picture shows a screen from Baird's original television presentation. The man in the picture is Baird's business partner.*

The Cathode Ray Tube

The next important step was made by an American named Philo T. Farnsworth. After graduating from university, Farnsworth got a grant from a businessman who hoped this genius could invent something that would make them money. He did. The invention was the **cathode ray tube**. This is the picture tube used in TV and computer screens before flat screen TVs.

Mahogany—the wood of mo introduce Farnsworth's advanc today appointed in the moder a television unit offering unsu dependability and maximum its best—from Farnsworth—

Philo T. Farnsworth

Farnsworth (1906–1971) was born in a Utah log cabin built by his father. He was the eldest of five children. His family was very poor, but his parents still sent their children to school. Farnsworth's best subjects were chemistry and physics. He put himself through university by working on a railroad.

Farnsworth patented his invention in 1927. He expected people to use it to watch symphonies and movies from their own homes. He couldn't have guessed at just how important television would become. Today, millions of people tune in to watch entertainment programs, news, and educational shows. When world leaders speak, they appear on television. When police need help, they send out a TV message.

In 1948, only one in every ten homes had a television. Today, the average North American household has three TVs.

The First Television

This brochure advertises Farnsworth's television. A cathode ray tube is full of electric pulses. When the pulses hit the gas in the tube, light is produced. The light is interpreted on a TV monitor to create pictures.

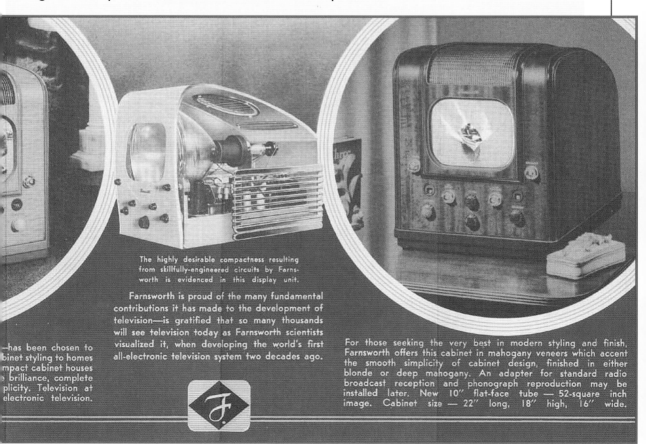

The highly desirable compactness resulting from skillfully-engineered circuits by Farnsworth is evidenced in this display unit.

Farnsworth is proud of the many fundamental contributions it has made to the development of television—is gratified that so many thousands will see television today as Farnsworth scientists visualized it, when developing the world's first all-electronic television system two decades ago.

–has been chosen to binet styling to homes mpact cabinet houses brilliance, complete plicity. Television at electronic television.

For those seeking the very best in modern styling and finish, Farnsworth offers this cabinet in mahogany veneers which accent the smooth simplicity of cabinet design, finished in either blonde or deep mahogany. An adapter for standard radio broadcast reception and phonograph reproduction may be installed later. New 10" flat-face tube — 52-square inch image. Cabinet size — 22" long, 18" high, 16" wide.

CHAPTER FIVE

The Computer in Today's World

In the past 100 years, technology has changed more than in the whole of human history before that. It doesn't show signs of slowing down either. Among the thousands of inventions, discoveries, and innovations used for communication, it is the computer that defines the modern world.

Today's computers are incredible machines that can do just about anything. They can play games, store information, and create art. They also help scientists speed up the process of invention.

The first computers were mechanical adding machines. It took a British code breaker and American ingenuity to develop

the device you know today. Then the military and scientists provided new ways of using it. Thanks to them, we can research on the Internet, email, and tweet one another.

The most recent innovation involves connecting a computer to the human brain. Who knows what might come next!

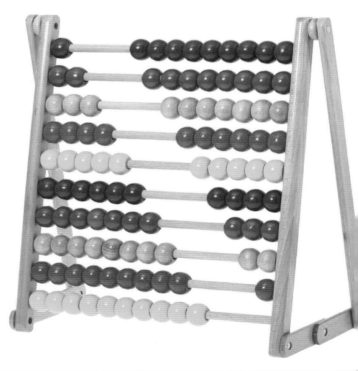

→ *The abacus is a non-mechanical computer. Some abacuses date as far back as ancient Mesopotamia.*

→ Babbage designed but never built a Difference Engine. This Difference Engine in the Science Museum in London, England, was built using his design.

The First Computers

For most of history, mathematicians did calculations in their head. This worked fine for small computations. Gigantic ones took great amounts of time, sometimes years. There was also the chance of making a simple calculation error.

The first computers were designed as giant calculators. That's where the name comes from. Computer means "something that computes or figures out an amount."

Charles Babbage and the Difference Engine

The first computer was Charles Babbage's **Difference Engine**. Babbage (1791–1871) was born in Surrey, England. He was the son of a wealthy banker and went to the best schools.

Although he was a poor student, he loved math. He didn't like going to class and preferred to teach himself. Babbage liked math so much that he decided to become a math professor. While studying towards this goal, he realized that it would be easier if he had a machine to help him calculate large numbers faster. He began developing a device that would mechanically add and subtract.

Although it took years, he finished his first design in 1821. Babbage called it the Difference Engine. Later, he built a more complex engine that was **programmable**. It was able to store numbers and remember them. Babbage's design is still the basic model for modern day computers.

↑ *Female secret agents played an important role during World War II. Here, some work with Turing's Colossus.*

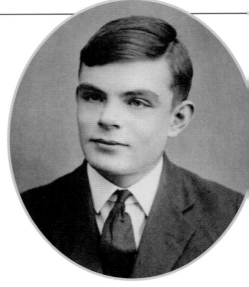

↑ *Alan Turing at the age of 16, 11 years before he joined the code breakers in Britain's secret service.*

Computers as Code Breakers

Babbage's Difference Engine was mechanical but not electrical. Electric computers trace their origins to a mathematician named Alan Turing (1912–1954). Turing was born in London, England. He had trouble making friends, but loved math. During World War II, the British government asked him to use his mathematical skill to help decode messages the Germans were sending.

Mathematicians are good at cracking codes because codes are based on algebra. Algebra uses symbols for numbers. You solve the equation to determine what number the symbol represents. Code breakers create equations for letters. Solving these

equations helps them figure out the code. In the 1930s, the Germans sent coded messages using their Enigma machine. The codes from this device were so difficult that Britain's top mathematicians failed to decipher them. In 1939, Turing joined the code breakers.

By 1940, he had developed a computer to help him solve his calculations. Called the *bombe*, this computer ran on both electricity and a motor. It quickly cracked the Enigma Code.

By 1943, the Germans had a second coding device. Turing built the Colossus computer to crack that one. Colossus was the first computer that plugged into the wall.

A Computer in Every Home

Like the word colossus suggests, the first computers were huge. They took up entire rooms. That changed in 1958 when an American engineer named Jack Kilby invented the **microchip**. Despite its small size, the microchip was able to store huge amounts of information.

Kilby (1923–2005) was born in Missouri. He loved science and eventually went to the University of Illinois, where he studied electrical engineering. Kilby was very interested in trying to make tiny electronic parts for computers.

↑ This shows the original size of Kilby's microchip, a tiny device that holds large amounts of computer coding.

After taking advanced courses, Kilby began working for Texas Instruments in 1958.

[This] was the only company that agreed to let me work on electronic component miniaturization more or less full time, and it turned out to be a great fit.

— Jack Kilby, Nobel biography, 2000

Through trial and error, Kilby came up with the microchip. In 1959, he filed a patent for his invention. In 2000, he won the Nobel Prize for developing it.

Today, microchips are so small that they can be placed under the skin of pets to identify them if they go missing.

Personal Computers

In the 1970s, personal computers went on the market. Thanks to the microchip, these computers were small enough to fit on a desk. They used a qwerty keyboard and had a screen with one of Farnsworth's cathode ray tubes. The keyboard and screen allowed users to write text, make calculations, and play simple games.

The popular Apple® computer was invented by Steve Wozniak (born 1950) in 1976. Douglas Engelbart (1925–2013) developed the popular Windows® **operating system** in the same year. Engelbart made the first computer mouse in 1963.

Early computers had an **interface** that used words on a screen. In 1973, a team of California computer scientists invented the Alto. This computer used pictures as its interface. The windows and icons on today's computers are all inspired by this system.

↓ *Kaypro computers such as this one were popular first computers. Notice the two drives. One of the drives held the program being used. The other held what was being typed.*

The World Wide Web

The invention of the Internet dramatically changed how we communicate. The original technology for the Internet was developed by the U.S. military to speed up communication. It took an inventor named Tim Berners-Lee (born 1955) to bring it to the public.

Berners-Lee was born in London, England, the son of two computer scientists. After graduating from Oxford University with a degree in physics, he worked for the European Organization for Nuclear Research. There he noticed how difficult it was to share information with scientists in different countries.

Berners-Lee wanted to create a way that scientists around the world could share documents. He developed a computer language called **hypertext mark-up language** or **HTML** in 1990. HTML is a code that tells computers what to put on their screens. For example, to tell the computer to make the color blue, HTML uses the code 0033FF.

Berners-Lee used HTML to make the first Web pages. His first page went online in 1991. Today, the Internet is part of everyday life for businesses and individuals.

↑ *In 2008, Berners-Lee created the Knight Foundation, an organization working to make the World Wide Web available free and to everyone.*

Email was invented in 1971 as a way for the military to send messages from computer to computer. The inventor, Ray Tomlinson (born 1941), also started using the @ symbol so that people would know who was at each computer. Before 1971, this symbol was often used to show prices, such as referring to 5 chocolate bars @ 75¢ each.

Smartphone Technology

In 1909, Nikola Tesla made the following prediction:

In the future it will only be necessary to carry an inexpensive instrument not bigger than a watch, which will enable its bearer to hear anywhere on sea or land for distances of thousands of miles. One may listen or transmit speech or song to the uttermost parts of the world.

↓ *Smartphones have decreased in size and increased in capabilities since 1992.*

That sounds pretty close to a modern-day **smartphone**. A smartphone is a mobile phone with a built-in computer. The first one was the Simon Personal Communicator made by IBM in 1992. Since then, smartphones have taken over the market. You can send emails, surf the Internet, and even make movies on them.

It's hard to say who invented the smartphone. In the past, it was possible for a single person to know enough about technology to invent a new device. Today, most inventions are made by groups of people working together. Many of them work for large companies.

→ This is what BCI looks like today. The contraption on the woman's head is a scanner that detects her brainwaves and translates them to the computer.

Brain-Computer Interface

First, the computer used a word-based interface. Today, it uses a picture-based interface. Some scientists believe that it will soon use a brain interface. A **brain-computer interface** is referred to as **BCI**. The technology is still in its experimental stage. Scientists have already hooked a person's brain directly to a computer. In the lab, test subjects have been able to control computers with their thoughts. Every day, scientists are getting closer to bringing BCI to the public.

Imagine how the idea might simplify your computer use. Consider how it might help those who are paralyzed or have arthritis. It could also help you do your homework much faster!

BCI
Building on the Work of Hans Berger

BCI is possible thanks to the work of Hans Berger (1873–1941). Berger discovered that the brain uses electrical impulses similar to those in a computer. In 1924, he was able to attach wires to a human brain and record the signals it made. This led to a branch of science called **electroencephalography**, which is the science of the brain's electric signals.

We've Come a Long Way

We've come a long way since cuneiform and papyrus. The way we communicate is faster and reaches farther than ever before. Almost anywhere in the world, the average person has access to more information every day than the most intelligent scholars of the ancient world could learn in a lifetime.

Some things stay the same. Although technology helps us communicate more easily, what we communicate is still the same as it was 6000 years ago. We want to tell our stories. We want to share with our friends and family. We want to learn and discover the world.

The Internet is a powerful tool. However, it can also be misused. It's important to learn how to read information properly so we can discriminate what's true from what's false. The latest smartphone can help you *find* what you're looking for, but it can't help you *know* what to look for. For that, we have to rely on the same things the Sumerians did—ourselves and our own brain.

So long as we do that, the future of communication is a bright one.

Learning More

Books

Freedman, Russell. *Out of Darkness: The Story of Louis Braille*. New York: Clarion Books, 1999.
Read about the young Frenchman who invented Braille.

no author. *Computer*.
New York: DK Publishing, 2011.
Find out about the many inventions that go together to make today's computer world.

Vander Hook, Sue. *Johannes Gutenberg: Printing Press Inventor*. Edina, Minnesota: ABDO Publishing Company, 2010.
Learn more about the life and work of the inventor of the printing press.

Walker, C.B.F. *Reading the Past: Cuneiform*. Berkeley, CA: University of California Press, 1987.
Learn about the earliest form of writing.

Websites

CERN **http://info.cern.ch/hypertext/WWW/TheProject.html**
See the world's first website.

ETV **http://www.knowitall.org/kidswork/index.html**
Click on the different buildings to open up links to learn about inventions.

PBS **http://www.pbs.org/tesla/**
See a program on Nikola Tesla.

Science Kids
http://www.sciencekids.co.nz/sciencefacts/scientists/alexandergrahambell.html
Learn more about Alexander Graham Bell.

Thomas Edison.com **http://www.thomasedison.com/**
Visit a website all about Thomas Edison.

YouTube **http://www.youtube.com/watch?v=uBL7V3zGMUA**
Hear the first recording of a human voice from 1860.

Timeline

BCE	
40,000	The first cave drawings are drawn.
4000	The Sumerians develop cuneiform writing.
3000	The Egyptians develop papyrus paper.
200	The Greeks develop parchment.
CE	
105	The Chinese make paper from rags and plant fibers.
200	The Romans develop the modern book, called a codex.
800s	An Arab scholar builds the first camera.
1041–1048	The Chinese invent the first moveable-type printing press.
1440	Johannes Gutenberg invents the first European printing press.
1794	Claude Chappe invents the mechanical telegraph.
1808	Pellegrino Turri invents the first typewriter.
1821	Louis Braille begins inventing the Braille alphabet. Charles Babbage designs the Difference Engine.
1824	Braille completes his alphabet.
1837	William Cooke and Charles Wheatstone build the electric telegraph. Samuel Morse invents the Morse code telegraph.
1844	Morse sends the first telegraph message in his code.
1845	The electric telegraph is used to catch a criminal.
1849	Innocenzo Manzetti uses telegraph wires to make a toy robot talk.
1850s	Antonio Meucci invents the first telephone but doesn't patent it.
1873	Christopher Sholes invents the qwerty keyboard.
1876	Alexander Graham Bell tests and patents his telephone.
1877	Thomas Edison invents the phonograph.

1886	Heinrich Rudolf Hertz discovers radio waves.
1888	George Eastman invents celluloid film.
1889	Edison also makes a movie camera with a built-in projector.
1892	Auguste and Louis Lumière build their own movie camera.
1895	The Lumière brothers start making movies to entertain people.
1897	Nikola Tesla applies to patent the first radio.
1898	Tesla uses radio waves to control a toy boat.
1900	Guglielmo Marconi patents his radio.
1901	Marconi makes the first long-distance radio transmission.
1906	Reginald Fessenden makes the first voice radio broadcast.
1918	Arthur Scherbius invents a coding machine later called the Enigma machine.
1924	Hans Berger records the signals the brain makes.
1926	John Baird gives the first public demonstration of the television.
1927	Philo T. Farnsworth patents the electric television.
1940	Alan Turing develops a computer called the *bombe*.
1943	Turing builds the first electric computer.
1958	Jack Kilby invents the microchip.
1963	Douglas Engelbart makes the first computer mouse.
1971	Ray Tomlinson invents email.
1973	Martin D. Cooper creates a telephone that works through radio waves.
1976	Steve Wozniak invents the Apple® computer.
	Engelbart invents the Windows® operating system.
1991	Tim Berners-Lee uses HTML to launch the first website.
1992	Neil Papworth develops the technology for sending text messages.
2010	First iPad is released.
2013	Scientists work on a brain-computer interface.

Glossary

BCI See brain-computer interface

Braille alphabet A special alphabet for the blind that uses raised bumps to represent letters; invented by Louis Braille in 1821

brain-computer interface A device that hooks the human brain to a computer; also referred to as BCI

cathode ray tube A glass or metal tube full of electric pulses that produce light and color when the pulses hit the gas in the tube; invented by Philo T. Farnsworth in 1927 and used in TVs until the development of the flat screen TV

celluloid film Very thin plastic that can be used to take many photos quickly; invented by George Eastman in 1888

cinematoscope An update of the kinetoscope; built by the Lumière brothers in 1892

codex A modern style of book with a front and back cover and pages between the covers

communication The exchange of ideas, stories, and information

cuneiform The earliest form of written language; developed in Mesopotamia around 4000 BCE

diaphragm A thin sheet of material that vibrates with sound and can be used to record sounds

Difference Engine A giant, mechanical calculator, designed by Charles Babbage in 1821

discovery Refers to uncovering or revealing something new for the first time

electroencephalography The science of the brain's electric signals

electromagnetic field A field created when a magnetic field and an electric field are put together; also called radio waves

five-needle telegraph The early electric telegraph built by William Cooke and Charles Wheatstone in 1837; used an electric pulse to move five needles on a sheet of paper to send messages

HTML See hypertext mark-up language

hypertext mark-up language A special computer code that tells a computer what to display on its screen; also known as HTML

innovation Refers to the improvement of an existing process, machine, or device

interface The way people communicate with computers

invention Refers to the first development of a process, machine, or device

kinetoscope An early movie camera made by Thomas Edison in 1889; included a built-in projector

microchip A miniature computer part able to store huge amounts of information

Morse code A system of dots and dashes used to transmit messages; developed in 1837 by Samuel Morse

papyrus The earliest form of paper made from dried leaves of the papyrus plant and invented by the Egyptians around 3000 BCE

operating system The software that makes a computer work

parchment A form of paper made from dried animal skins that have been stretched after the hair has been removed; invented by the ancient Greeks around 200 BCE

patent An official document that gives an inventor the right to make, use, or sell an invention

phonograph A machine that used wax cylinders to record and reproduce sound; invented by Thomas Edison in 1877

photography The process of taking pictures

printing press A machine used to make multiple copies of a piece of writing; first invented by the Chinese; in 1440 Johannes Gutenberg invented the first European one

programmable Description of a device that can store and remember numbers and other information

radio waves Invisible electromagnetic waves used to transmit signals

scribes People in ancient societies who could read and write and who worked copying out documents

scrolls An early version of a book consisting of long pieces of parchment or paper rolled up

semaphore A method of communication using long, mechanical wooden arms on a tower to transmit messages; invented by Claude Chappe in 1794

smartphone A cell phone with a built-in computer

stylus A Thin, pencil-like writing implement made from a piece of reed or bamboo

technologies The use of scientific discoveries to create tools to solve problems

telegraph A device for transmitting and receiving messages from a distance, usually along a wire

telegraphy The study of using or making systems to communicate information

text A piece of writing

Index